CRIME
SCIENCE

TERRORISM

Matt Anniss

Gareth Stevens
Publishing

Please visit our website, www.garethstevens.com. For a free color catalog of all our high-quality books, call toll free 1-800-542-2595 or fax 1-877-542-2596.

Library of Congress Cataloging-in-Publication Data

Anniss, Matt.
Terrorism / by Matt Anniss.
  p. cm. — (Crime science)
Includes index.
ISBN 978-1-4339-9497-5 (pbk.)
ISBN 978-1-4339-9498-2 (6-pack)
ISBN 978-1-4339-9496-8 (library binding)
1. Terrorism — Juvenile literature. 2. Terrorism — Prevention — Juvenile literature. 3. Terrorists — Juvenile literature. I. Anniss, Matt. II. Title.
HV6431.A56 2014
303.6—dc23

First Edition

Published in 2014 by
Gareth Stevens Publishing
111 East 14th Street, Suite 349
New York, NY 10003

© 2014 Gareth Stevens Publishing

Produced by Calcium, www.calciumcreative.co.uk
Designed by Keith Williams and Paul Myerscough
Edited by Sarah Eason and Jennifer Sanderson

Photo credits: Cover: Shutterstock: Arindambanerjee b, Fernando Cortes tl, Larry Bruce tr. Inside: Dreamstime: 36clicks 38t, Ahmet Ihsan Ariturk 7t, Ivan Cholakov 20, Cozyta 14, Konstantin32 32, Carolina K. Smith M.d. 17, Tomasz Szymanski 35b, Oleg Zabielin 8; Shutterstock: 1000 Words 5tr, 18percentgrey 30, AlexKalashnikov 1, 24, Asianet-Pakistan 28, Yuri Bathan 21b, Franck Boston 33t, Stephen Bures 23, Larry Bruce 45, Konstantin Chagin 41b, ChameleonsEye 22, Anthony Correia 27, Mehmet Dilsiz 7b, Dotshock 15, Edobric 6, Edw 4, Jack Dagley Photography 13b, Jose Gil 11, Pashin Georgiy 31b, Homeros 9, 10b, 25t, Brendan Howard 10t, Hurricanehank 12, i4lcocl2 35t, ID1974 19, Anna Jurkovska 34, Jan Kranendonk 43, Marco Mayer 40, Katarzyna Mazurowska 44, Michaeljung 21t, Phoenix79 26, Pressmaster 16t, 18, Przemek Tokar 33b, RTimages 25b, Rena Schild 41t, Spirit of America 13t, James Steidl 38b, Leah-Anne Thompson 29, Tifonimages 37, Monika Wisniewska 39, Mateusz Wolski 36, YanLev 42, Lisa F. Young 5cl; Wikimedia Commons: Juan de Vojníkov 31t, Israel Defense Forces 16b.

Printed in the United States of America

CPSIA compliance information: Batch #CS13GS: For further information contact Gareth Stevens, New York, New York at 1-800-542-2595.

CONTENTS

TERRORISM

If you watch or listen to the news, there is a strong chance that there will be a report on a terrorist attack somewhere in the world. It could be a suicide bombing in Israel, a car bomb in Afghanistan, or even a mass shooting in a sleepy European town. Terrorism has no borders—it is just as much a problem in the United States as it is in the Middle East.

Acts of Terror

Terrorism is any act made to cause fear through mass destruction and loss of life. It can be carried out by organized terrorist groups or disgruntled individuals. By mid-2012 alone, there were nearly 180 terrorist attacks around the world, resulting in the loss of thousands of lives.

Forensic scientists play a huge part in investigating deadly acts of terrorism.

Constant Battle

Protecting the public from acts of terrorism is very complicated. Terrorists are often individuals who try to keep their plans secret, so governments spend billions of dollars every year working to prevent terrorist attacks. Science is very important in fighting this "war on terror." The work of forensic scientists helps governments stay one step ahead of the terrorists.

Security measures have been developed to protect the public from terrorist attacks.

Following a terrorist attack, every shred of evidence is scientifically tested.

BACK IN THE LAB

In the United States, both the FBI and the CIA have a role to play in stopping possible terrorist attacks. Counterterrorism agents act as a bridge between the police, government, and intelligence agencies. They keep close track of the latest scientific and political developments, and offer advice on how best to deal with the terrorist threat to US interests around the world.

CHAPTER ONE
THE WAR ON TERROR

Before terrorists can be stopped in their tracks, investigators have to know who they are and what motivates them. Learning this is one of the key jobs of the group of forensic scientists and special agents who work in counterterrorism.

What Is Counterterrorism?

Counterterrorism is anything done to "counter" the terrorist threat to a particular country. This means preventing acts of terrorism, capturing terrorists, and investigating terrorist attacks.

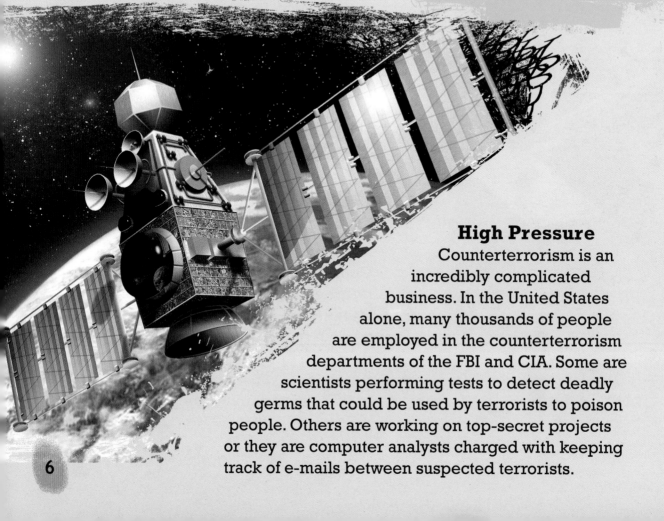

Spy satellites are one of the US government's biggest weapons in the war on terror.

High Pressure

Counterterrorism is an incredibly complicated business. In the United States alone, many thousands of people are employed in the counterterrorism departments of the FBI and CIA. Some are scientists performing tests to detect deadly germs that could be used by terrorists to poison people. Others are working on top-secret projects or they are computer analysts charged with keeping track of e-mails between suspected terrorists.

Difficult Job

Working in counterterrorism is a high-pressure job. A single mistake could result in a terrorist attack that kills hundreds or thousands of people.

One Step Ahead

Terrorists are constantly coming up with new ways to make deadly weapons, so counterterrorism workers need to stay ahead of their enemy. Terrorists also do everything they can to avoid detection, so counterterrorism officials face a constant battle to uncover their plans.

Terrorists do their best to blend into the crowd, in order to avoid detection.

BACK IN THE LAB

Counterterrorism scientists work specifically on projects linked to the threat of terrorism. Some scientists are charged with discovering new, cutting-edge forensic techniques to help in the detection of planned attacks. Others carry out research into chemicals that could be used as weapons. Their work is highly secretive, but vital to ensure our safety.

Cell phone conversations can be monitored by counterterrorism agents.

HOLY WAR

Many terrorist attacks are carried out in the name of religion. There are people around the world who believe they are in a "holy war" against those with different religious views. Often, they are prepared to die for their extreme religious beliefs and, because of this, they are very dangerous.

In the Name of Religion

Many of the most deadly terror attacks the world has ever seen have been the work of religious extremists. The 9/11 attacks, the most high-profile terrorist act on US soil, were the work of a small group of people who believe in an extreme form of Islam.

War Against the West

The "fundamentalists" who were responsible for the 9/11 attacks were part of a terrorist organization, called Al-Qaeda. One of Al-Qaeda's aims is to wage war against the West, especially Christian and Jewish people.

The tension between religions in the Middle East has inspired many acts of terrorism.

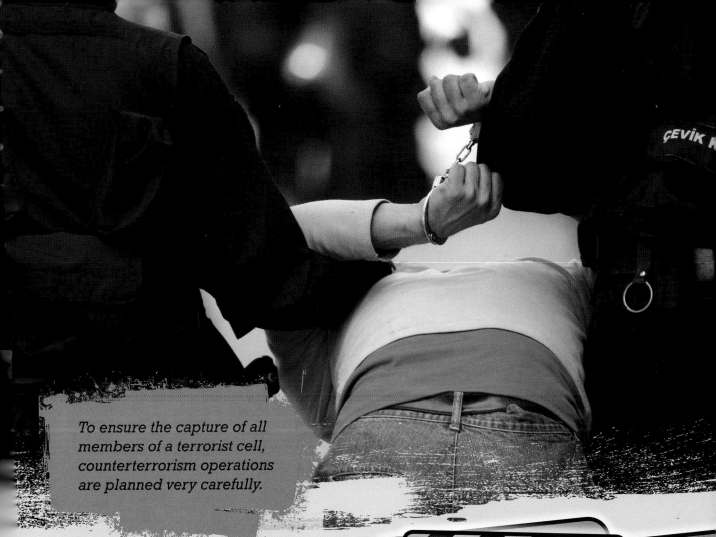

To ensure the capture of all members of a terrorist cell, counterterrorism operations are planned very carefully.

The Enemy Within

Terrorists are often organized into cells. These are groups that plan and carry out attacks. The methods used in these attacks vary, from hijacking planes to taking hostages, but most include the use of homemade bombs.

Homemade Bombs

Bombs are often made from household items. Finding terror cells, and working out how they plan to make bombs, are two of the biggest challenges facing counterterrorism officials.

REAL-LIFE CASE

In 2006, a Lebanese man called Assem Hammoud was arrested by the FBI. Hammoud was behind a plot to blow up subway tunnels under the Hudson River in New York. The FBI uncovered the plot after discovering and decoding secret messages left by Hammoud on Internet message boards.

STANDING UP FOR A CAUSE

Not all terrorists are religious extremists. Some hold extreme political views or are motivated to plan acts of terror by their belief in a particular cause. In the United States, these kinds of terrorists are not as high profile but they may still exist. Around the world, they are far more common.

Political Terrorism

Terrorism inspired by politics has been around for nearly 100 years. The most famous example is the IRA, an organization dedicated to freeing Northern Ireland from British rule. Until the IRA called a ceasefire in 1997, it was responsible for countless terror attacks.

Fighting for Freedom

In 2011, a terrorist organization called ETA called off its long-running struggle against Spanish rule of the Basque region of Spain. Between 1968 and 2011, their attacks claimed the lives of more than 800 people.

Terror groups in Northern Ireland boasted about their strength by painting murals on the side of buildings.

Many cities have suffered huge damage as a result of political terrorist groups.

Animal rights attacks against scientists became so common in 2009 that demonstrators took to the streets in Los Angeles.

CRACKED
When investigating letter-bomb attacks by animal rights separatists, police and forensic scientists will dust for fingerprints and test for traces of DNA. They also closely monitor Internet communications between animal rights activists.

Several Steps Too Far

There are many smaller terror groups around the world who gain inspiration from extreme views or their belief in a particular cause. For example, the FBI monitors white separatist groups in the United States who are motivated by hatred of black people. The Animal Rights Militia and Animal Liberation Front have both carried out terrorist acts in the name of protecting animals that are used in scientific research. Many scientists who work in animal-testing laboratories have been harmed by letter bombs sent to their homes in the United States, Canada, and the United Kingdom.

11

THE LONE WOLF

Although terrorist groups are secretive, it is possible to uncover their plans by monitoring their e-mails or placing undercover agents within the cells. But when terrorists act alone, this is often not possible. Because of this, uncovering their plans and stopping them can prove incredibly difficult.

Complicated Reasons

Counterterrorism operatives call a terrorist who acts alone a "lone wolf." Unlike those involved with organized terror groups, lone-wolf terrorists do not always have straightforward motivations.

Protests

Timothy McVeigh, the man behind the 1995 Oklahoma City bombing, told the FBI that he carried out the attack as a protest against the government. Ted Kaczynski, better known as the Unabomber, carried out a nationwide campaign of attacks between 1978 and 1995 as a protest against modern technology.

It can be difficult to uncover the unusual and unpredictable plans of lone wolf terrorists.

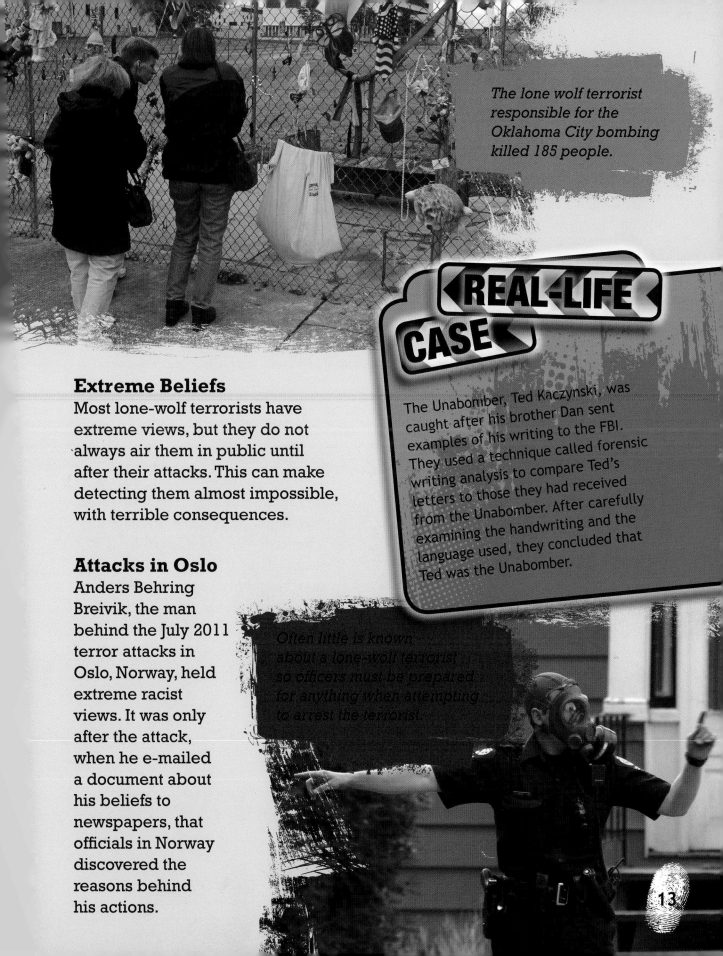

The lone wolf terrorist responsible for the Oklahoma City bombing killed 185 people.

Extreme Beliefs

Most lone-wolf terrorists have extreme views, but they do not always air them in public until after their attacks. This can make detecting them almost impossible, with terrible consequences.

Attacks in Oslo

Anders Behring Breivik, the man behind the July 2011 terror attacks in Oslo, Norway, held extreme racist views. It was only after the attack, when he e-mailed a document about his beliefs to newspapers, that officials in Norway discovered the reasons behind his actions.

REAL-LIFE CASE

The Unabomber, Ted Kaczynski, was caught after his brother Dan sent examples of his writing to the FBI. They used a technique called forensic writing analysis to compare Ted's letters to those they had received from the Unabomber. After carefully examining the handwriting and the language used, they concluded that Ted was the Unabomber.

Often little is known about a lone-wolf terrorist so officers must be prepared for anything when attempting to arrest the terrorist.

13

CHAPTER TWO
COUNTERTERRORISM

One of the highest priorities of counterterrorism agents around the world is preventing terrorist attacks. To help do this, they use a range of high-tech scientific techniques.

Watching the Internet

The Internet revolution of the last 20 years has made it possible for people all over the world to be connected to each other. It has also made it possible for terrorists scattered in remote places around the world to plan attacks, away from the prying eyes of counterterrorism agents.

Huge Task

Due to the increased threat of terrorism attacks in recent years, government counterterrorism agencies devote a lot of time to monitoring the Internet. This can take many forms, from checking websites run by fundamentalists to monitoring online sales of materials used in the making of homemade bombs.

Al-Qaeda terrorists often keep in contact by e-mail or by using coded language on Internet message boards.

Key Techniques

Counterterrorism agents use special techniques, called "traffic analysis" and "packet sniffing," to monitor the online discussions of suspected terrorists. Traffic analysis means watching the frequency of e-mails between two or more suspected terrorists in order to figure out what they are up to. If a lot of e-mails are sent and received in a short space of time, it could mean that an attack is being planned. As the Internet is so vast, monitoring the activities of suspected terrorists is a huge task.

CRACKED

Government counterterrorism agents regularly use packet sniffing to monitor communications across the Internet. Packet sniffing, also sometimes called packet analyzing, involves using computer software to track and record everything that passes across a selected computer network (for example, those used by people to access the Internet at home or on the move). By doing this, counterterrorism agents can keep an eye out for e-mails from suspected terrorists.

The CIA uses banks of computer servers to store and analyze e-mails from suspected terrorists.

WATCHING THE TERRORISTS

Once a suspected or known terrorist has been identified, counterterrorism agents will use all the scientific tools they have to keep track of them. This can mean using surveillance techniques previously used only by the armed services.

Listening Intently

The armed services have access to powerful tools that they use to watch and track terrorists. This is called surveillance. The US government has listening stations throughout the world. These use powerful listening devices to pick up cell phone calls and radio communications. The US government also uses satellites, positioned hundreds of miles above Earth, to film suspected terrorist activity.

Agents are trained to listen to radio communications and phone calls between suspected terrorists.

Pictures taken by satellites help counterterrorism officials to keep track of terrorist cells.

Global Positioning

Most modern cell phones regularly communicate with the Global Positioning System (GPS). This system is used by millions of people around the world every day and can also be used to monitor the movement of terrorists.

Finding Their Position

GPS allows electronic devices to calculate their exact position by sending and receiving signals to a network of satellites. If the cell phone number of a suspected terrorist is known, his or her movements can be tracked using the GPS network.

Despite using surveillance, it took the CIA years to track down and kill Osama Bin Laden.

REAL-LIFE CASE

The capturing and killing of Al-Qaeda leader Osama Bin Laden in May 2011 was the result of one of the biggest surveillance operations in US history. Over a period of around six months, the CIA used satellites and unmanned drone planes to film Bin Laden's home, a compound in Pakistan, from every possible angle. By doing this, they were not only able to identify everyone in the compound, but also plan the attack on Bin Laden in great detail.

SCOURING THE RECORDS

Counterterrorism agents watch the Internet to monitor the movements of terrorists. They also use a number of high-tech methods to keep track of telephone calls made and received by those suspected of being involved in terrorist activity.

Call Databases

Since 2001, the United States National Security Agency (NSA) has recorded basic details of all phone calls made and received by customers of the country's four biggest telephone companies. Details of numbers dialed, calls received, and call length are stored on a massive bank of computers in what is known as a call database. Counterterrorism agents use this to find out who is making and receiving calls from suspected terrorists.

Many agents spend most of their week listening to phone calls or trawling through e-mails from suspected terrorists.

Agents use custom-made surveillance kits to keep track of information while out in the field.

Registering Terrorist Activity

Call databases can be useful to counterterrorism agents, but their vast size makes them difficult to handle. This is why they also use pen registers. These monitor the calls made from a particular phone.

Collecting Evidence

During counterterrorism operations, wire-tapping devices may also be used. These can record phone conversations between suspected criminals or terrorists. Wire-tapping is usually used to collect evidence. Occasionally, video cameras or other recording devices may be placed in the homes of suspected terrorists.

BACK IN THE LAB

The CIA and FBI use pen registers to track the phone calls of suspected terrorists. A pen register records and decodes the numbers called by a particular fixed line or cell phone. Traditionally, pen registers are used with a trap-and-trace device. Trap-and-trace devices record the numbers dialed on a particular phone.

OUTWITTING THE TERRORISTS

The methods used by terrorists are constantly changing, so counterterrorism agents need to work on new and improved methods. These cutting-edge techniques are currently being worked on by some of the world's top scientists.

In the Laboratory

Governments invest millions of dollars every year in counterterrorism laboratories. These laboratories are places where some of the most talented scientists in the country spend hours researching new forensic techniques. These techniques will be used when investigating terrorist crimes and working on top-secret projects that could help to stop terrorist attacks before they happen.

In order to perfect their response, the US government often stages terrorist attacks during military training.

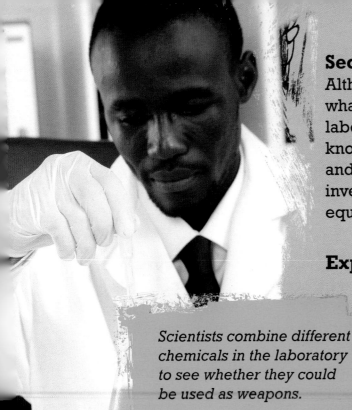

Secret Squirrels

Although it is impossible to find out exactly what the scientists in the counterterrorism laboratories are working on, we do now know that they work on new computer and communications systems, forensic investigation techniques, and developing equipment to be used by field agents.

Experimenting and Testing

Counterterrorism scientists carry out experiments to find out whether household items, such as soft-drink cans, batteries, and bleach, can be used to make bombs. They also refine and develop techniques, such as DNA and fingerprint testing.

Scientists combine different chemicals in the laboratory to see whether they could be used as weapons.

BACK IN THE LAB

One of the key areas of research carried out by counterterrorism labs is chemical analysis. This involves closely examining chemical substances, both natural and man-made, how they work, and if they could potentially be used in weapons. If a terrorist bomb attack is successful, forensic scientists often carry out a chemical analysis on remains to find out how the bomb was made.

Scientists examine microscopic evidence to discover how terrorists carried out an attack.

21

THE WAR ON INVISIBLE WEAPONS

Many counterterrorism officials think that the greatest terrorist threat in the future may not come from homemade bombs, but rather chemical and biological weapons. These include poisonous gases and deadly germs that could kill hundreds of thousands of people.

Gas Attack

It is not difficult to create poisonous gases in a laboratory, and the CIA believes that some terror groups may have this capability. They are not yet sure that terrorists are able to create germs that will make people very sick, but they have to be prepared for the possibility. For this reason, much of the work carried out in counterterrorism labs is dedicated to developing methods to deal with possible poison or germ gas attacks.

Investigators often wear protective suits to make sure they do not breathe in poisonous gases.

Germ Warfare

One of the problems facing
scientists is that germs and
poison gases are often
colorless and odorless.
If a terrorist released
germs or poison in a
crowded place, it would
be difficult to detect them.

Biodetectors

To help identify if gases
have been released,
scientists have developed
biodetectors. These are
chemicals that change
appearance if a certain gas
or germ is present. They can
be put inside devices carried
by field agents, so that the
agents can detect poison threats.

BACK
IN THE
LAB

Most biodetectors include some
kind of living organism—for example,
a germ—that changes its appearance
in the presence of a particular poison.
Biodetectors are far more sensitive
to poisonous substances than humans,
meaning they can detect them long
before they may do us any harm.

WEAPONS OF MASS DESTRUCTION

As well as researching chemical weapons, counterterrorism scientists also figure out what combination of household objects and chemicals could be used to create homemade bombs. To stop someone from making a bomb, you must know exactly how one can be created.

Devious Plans

By nature, terrorists can be extremely devious and they are always looking for new ways to create bombs. For example, in December 2001, a man was arrested on a flight from Paris, France, to Miami after attempting to blow up the plane using a bomb hidden in the sole of his shoe. Before this happened, counterterrorism scientists had never imagined that a terrorist would try this. It proved that in order to prevent terrorism attacks, scientists need to think like terrorists.

Terrorists, especially in the Middle East, often plant bombs inside cars or vans.

Counterterrorism officials have developed high-tech robots to help bomb-disposal experts.

Tiny Weapons

The CIA believes that organized terror groups may attempt to use nanotechnology to create bombs. Nanotechnology is the science of things so small that they can be seen only under microscopes.

At present, this is a highly unlikely scenario. However, because it may be possible in the future, the US government is funding research into the development of nanotech weapons. If terrorists use nanotechnology, the government hopes to be able to foil their plans.

Scientists work hard testing out different combinations of chemicals to attempt to outwit terrorists.

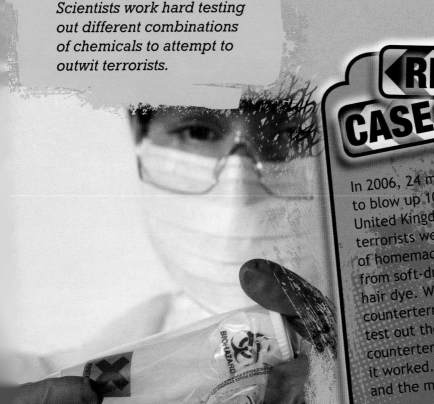

REAL-LIFE CASE

In 2006, 24 men were arrested for planning to blow up 10 planes traveling from London, United Kingdom, to the United States. The terrorists were hoping to use a new type of homemade bomb. Their bomb was made from soft-drink bottles, batteries, and hair dye. When the plot was uncovered, counterterrorism officials decided to test out the terrorists' bomb design in a counterterrorism laboratory to see whether it worked. Their "test bombs" exploded and the men were arrested.

CHAPTER THREE

INVESTIGATING TERRORIST ATTACKS

Although counterterrorism agents work incredibly hard to prevent terrorist attacks, they are not always successful. If a terrorist attack takes place, it is the role of crime scene investigators, federal agents, and forensic scientists to attempt to figure out what happened, why it happened, and who was behind it.

The Job Nobody Wants

Whether they are police officers, federal agents, or forensic scientists, nobody wants to have to investigate a terrorist attack. If they are sent to the scene of a terrorist attack, there is a strong chance that many people will have been killed or injured. Crime scene investigators will also be under pressure to work quickly to get results as fast as possible.

It can take weeks or months for investigators to sift through the wreckage after a serious terrorist attack.

Results Needed

Investigating a terrorist attack can take a long time. If many people have died, counterterrorism scientists will need to look for evidence that will help them to determine how each person died.

Looking for Clues

Investigators also look for clues that could show how the attack was carried out. For example, was it a bombing, and if so, what was used to make the bomb? Were the terrorists killed in the attack, or are they still at large?

Relentless Task

When investigating acts of terrorism, counterterrorism scientists need to find evidence that will lead them to those behind the attacks. In extreme circumstances, such as those surrounding the attacks on the World Trade Center, they may also need to use all of their scientific skills to identify victims. Many of the methods they use are similar to those of regular forensic scientists. However, the nature of terrorist crimes means there are also additional scientific methods at their disposal.

Firefighters must secure the scene of a terrorist attack, putting out any fires, before investigators can begin their work.

CRACKED

When arriving at the scene of a terrorist attack, counterterrorism scientists must carefully examine the crime scene. If it has been a particularly large attack, this may take days, weeks, or even months. They will take photographs and carefully collect evidence before taking it to a laboratory for testing.

27

SIFTING THROUGH THE WRECKAGE

When an explosion takes place, counterterrorism scientists must act quickly to determine the cause. Sometimes, explosions occur naturally, for example following a gas leak. Occasionally, a bomb planted by a terrorist is the cause. Whatever the cause, counterterrorism scientists must find out what happened and why it happened.

Looking Carefully

Some scientists specialize in explosives. After a terrorist bomb blast, they will look for evidence to find out what caused the explosion. The area around the bomb site will be carefully examined for fragments, or pieces, of the bomb, gunpowder dust, traces of explosive, and wires and elements that could have been used to make a timing device. Marks on rubble and nearby structures can also be used to help pinpoint the exact location where the bomb was placed and detonated.

Even though they are trained and experienced in the field, it can take investigators a long time to fully search a bomb site.

Laboratory Testing

Forensic scientists must collect as much evidence as they can to take back to the laboratory. Once there, any fragments found will be tested to work out exactly what was used to make the bomb. These fragments will also be examined to see if they contain the bomber's fingerprints or DNA. Forensic methods are now so advanced that it is sometimes even possible to figure out exactly where and when the bomb was made.

Any evidence found at a bomb site must be bagged and noted as part of a criminal investigation.

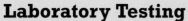
When investigating the first bombing of the World Trade Center in 1993, forensic scientists found a tiny piece of an axle from a van. From this they deduced that the bomb had been placed inside the van. On further inspection, they found that there was a vehicle identification number on the axle fragment. This allowed them to not only trace the van back to a car rental station in New Jersey, but also to the terrorist who had rented it.

THE IMPORTANCE OF DNA

Another amazing tool available to counterterrorism scientists is DNA testing. This is the most accurate and advanced identification system. It is said to be accurate in 99 percent of cases. This means that, should DNA evidence exist, it is almost impossible for a criminal or terrorist to escape identification.

Our Personal Pincode

DNA is a unique code that exists in every human body cell. Every single person's DNA is different and it is impossible to fake. Traces of DNA can be found in body parts, hair, teeth, and the tiny skin cells left by terrorists at crime scenes.

If a suspected terrorist is arrested, the police will carry out a DNA test to determine whether it matches any traces of DNA found at the crime scene or bomb site. In cases where the terrorist has died in the bomb blast, DNA can also be used to identify him or her.

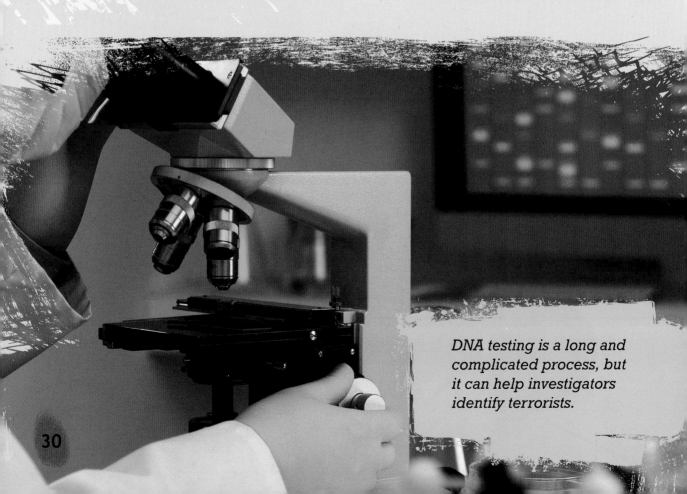

DNA testing is a long and complicated process, but it can help investigators identify terrorists.

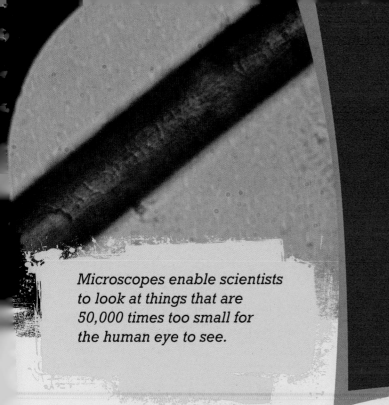

Microscopes enable scientists to look at things that are 50,000 times too small for the human eye to see.

CRACKED

DNA testing on human remains found in the aftermath of the 9/11 attacks in New York has helped to identify 1,633 of the estimated 2,753 people who died. In the months following the attack, DNA was taken from surviving family members and used to match the remains of victims. More than 10 years after the attacks took place, victims are still being identified using DNA analysis.

The Appliance of Science

It is also possible to identify human remains, such as bones and teeth, using a process called mitochondrial DNA testing. This can be very useful to counterterrorism scientists when the fire following a bomb blast has destroyed most of the evidence. Mitochondrial DNA testing is a very slow process, and is nowhere near as accurate as regular DNA testing. However, it is accurate enough to identify missing people following a terrorist attack.

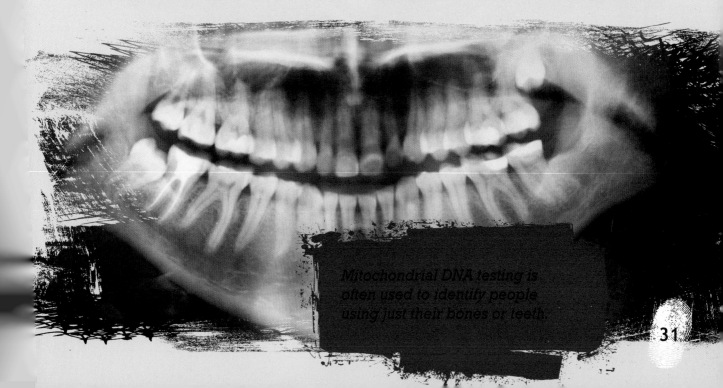

Mitochondrial DNA testing is often used to identify people using just their bones or teeth.

BIOMETRIC MATTERS

DNA testing is not the only way of identifying suspected terrorists. In recent years, resources have been invested in "biometrics." This is the use of human characteristics to identify people using photographs and film. When DNA evidence is not available, biometrics can be extremely valuable to counterterrorism agents.

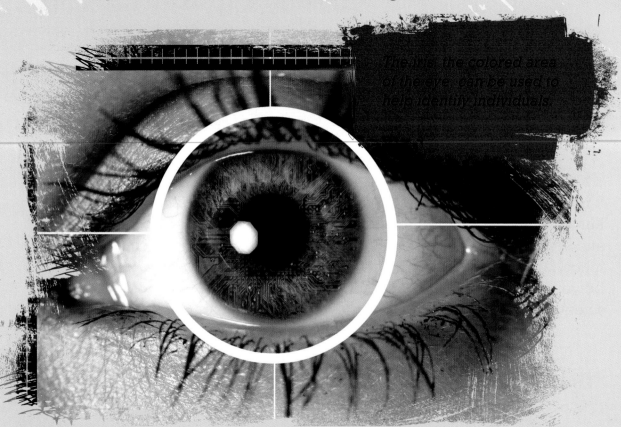

The iris, the colored area of the eye, can be used to help identify individuals.

Passport Photos

The most common application of biometrics is in passports. For example, all US and British passports issued today include a microchip that stores statistics about the passport holder's facial features, such as the shape of his or her face, length of nose, eye color, and so on. Some airports now make people walk through biometric scanners on arrival, to make sure that the person entering the country is who they say they are. In addition, a photograph is now taken of everyone who enters the United States. This is kept on record for 75 years and can be used to make a biometric profile if needed.

Identifying Suspects

The development of biometrics has allowed counterterrorism agents to accurately identify terrorism suspects from a distance, using surveillance cameras and satellite images.

Checking Suspects

If there is a picture of a terror suspect on file, it can be cross-checked with a new photograph or film footage. This technique is used by the military when identifying terrorism suspects in countries such as Pakistan and Afghanistan.

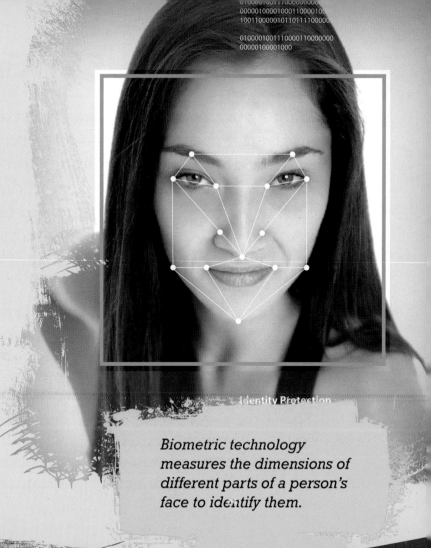

Biometric technology measures the dimensions of different parts of a person's face to identify them.

Biometric technology helps soldiers to identify known terrorists in Afghanistan.

CRACKED

Cutting-edge biometric identification techniques were used in the hunt to find and kill Osama Bin Laden. Before ordering the raid on Bin Laden's compound, the CIA cross-checked satellite images of the residents of the compound with pictures they had on file of Bin Laden. Once Bin Laden was killed, a soldier took a picture of him to make sure that the man they had killed was in fact the terrorist leader himself.

AIR-CRASH INVESTIGATION

Some of the worst terrorist attacks of recent years have involved aircraft. Terrorists often target planes because they are unprotected, and when they crash, it is likely that hundreds of people will die. When a terrorist causes a plane to explode or crash, it is the work of aircraft-accident investigators to piece together what happened and why it happened.

Find the Box

Investigations into aircraft accidents and crashes within the United States are the responsibility of the National Transportation Safety Board. They have a team of experts who examine all available evidence to determine the cause of any incidents, whether deadly or not.

The first task for the investigators is to recover the flight recorder and cabin voice recorder. These two steel boxes are fitted to each aircraft and should contain all the information needed to figure out whether an airplane was hijacked or bombed, or if it crashed due to technical failure.

Flight recorders help determine what happened in the event of a crash or terrorist attack.

Reconstruction

Even when investigators know that an airplane has been bombed, they still need to piece together the exact details of how the explosion happened and destroyed the plane. In this instance, they often try to recover as much wreckage as possible to examine it for clues. If an airplane crashes over water, this is often not possible. Then, focus will switch back to finding the flight recorder, which may be the only means of finding out what happened.

Although terrorists often target planes, successful attacks are still a rarity.

REAL-LIFE CASE

After an airplane exploded over the town of Lockerbie in Scotland in 1988, air-crash investigators collected the wreckage and transported it to a hangar in England. There, they were able to put the plane back together, piece-by-piece. When they did this, they discovered a hole 66 feet (20 m) wide in the underside of the front cargo hold. From this, they deduced that a bomb had been placed in a suitcase.

If a plane crashes into the ground, investigators may find it hard to piece together what happened.

CHAPTER FOUR
KEEPING US SAFE

Science plays an important role in preventing terrorism and investigating terrorist attacks. It is also the driving force behind inventions and techniques that keep us safe from harm.

The Enemy Within

If you were asked to describe a typical terrorist, where would you begin? One of the most difficult aspects of terrorist control is that terrorists appear to be ordinary people who are going about everyday lives. Terrorists live within the countries they wish to attack, within their communities. They are highly organized and can change their plans at speed to outwit counterterrorism units. This is why it is so hard to control terrorism.

Armed police response teams are trained to know what to do in the event of a terrorist attack.

Cat and Mouse

Most terrorists and terror groups cannot afford to spend the vast amount of money that governments can invest in scientific research. However, that does not mean that they cannot come up with complex bomb plots or develop new weapons using cutting-edge scientific techniques.

Beating the Authorities

Terrorists are always looking for any weaknesses within a country's defenses, whether they are at airports, stadiums, or shopping malls. To prevent attacks, agents must predict possible terrorist actions.

Step By Step

Government agencies and private firms spend billions of dollars every year on scientific research programs into key areas of counterterrorism. Because of this, every year new inventions are unveiled to improve security. Meanwhile, scientists are constantly perfecting new methods of searching the Internet for information about planned terrorist activity. Counterterrorism agencies also use horizon scanning, which is the process of predicting future scientific developments.

CRACKED

In the summer of 2012, the US government unveiled its latest weapon in the "war on terror." It was a robotic device called SAPBER (Semi Autonomous Pipe Bomb End-cap Remover). The SAPBER has been designed to dismantle dangerous pipe bombs and to then collect vital evidence.

Airport security has been tightened in response to the increased threat of terrorism worldwide.

37

SECURITY TO SAVE US

Since traveling on airplanes first became popular in the early 1970s, terrorists have chosen to target airliners. Many of the worst terrorist attacks of the last 40 years have involved terrorists either blowing up, crashing, or hijacking planes. As a result, billions of dollars have been spent on airport security in order to keep passengers safe.

Every piece of luggage must be carefully searched before it is allowed on a plane.

Metal detectors are designed to stop terrorists from taking deadly weapons onto aircraft.

Tight Security

Up until 1972, it was possible to board a plane without having any bags checked. Then, following a high-profile terrorist hijacking, the US government ordered all US airports to install metal detectors. Nowadays, airport security is tighter than ever before. X-ray machines, based on those used in hospitals to check for broken bones, allow security staff to look inside bags without opening them. In 2009, scientists launched their newest device to tackle terrorism: the full-body scanner.

Scanning for Weapons

Full-body scanner machines use invisible radio waves to create a three-dimensional computer image. By doing this, security staff can see whether travelers are hiding drugs, weapons, and explosives. This is just one example of how airport security is responding to the threat of terrorism. In 2006, the CIA uncovered a plot to use plastic bottles in a terrorist attack. Since then, it has been illegal to carry plastic bottles of more than 3.4 fluid ounces (100 ml) onto an airplane.

REAL-LIFE CASE

The continued importance of airport security was revealed in May 2012. A man carrying a bomb was arrested in Yemen while on his way to catch a plane bound for the United States. The bomb, which was more advanced than the CIA had previously seen, was sewn inside the terrorist's underwear.

Airport "sniffer" dogs are trained to sniff out explosives, drugs, and firearms.

HORIZON SCANNING

The worlds of science and technology change so quickly that it is difficult to keep up. To ensure that they stay one step ahead of the terrorists, governments throughout the world need to make sure they keep abreast of all developments, however small. Because of this, they employ people called horizon scanners.

Simple Concept

The concept of "horizon scanning" is simple. It means closely watching scientific developments in order to predict future discoveries. For example, if one group of scientists discovers a new type of chemical, horizon-scanning experts would note this and think about how it might be used in the future. It could be that the chemical has potential to be used to make a bomb. It is the job of horizon scanners to figure this out before any terrorists do.

Horizon-scanning experts must keep up to date with all the latest scientific developments.

Complicated Business

Horizon scanning is now an essential part of counterterrorism. Although keeping up with new scientific research is a key element of it, some horizon scanners also specialize in other aspects of counterterrorism. Some may be specialists in global affairs and politics, for example, while others will focus on the Internet and computer technology. Gathering as much informtion as possible will help the government prevent terrorism in the future and bring those involved to justice.

Horizon-scanning experts advise President Obama on developments in terrorism and counterterrorism.

Horizon-scanning specialists do a huge amount of research in order to stay on top of developments.

BACK IN THE LAB

According to government sources, counterterrorism horizon scanners divide their time between reading reports from scientists, gathering information from counterterrorism agents, and writing advice for the government.

41

CYBER CHALLENGES

The growth of the World Wide Web and the use of personal Internet devices, such as smartphones and tablet computers, is a huge problem for computer scientists specializing in counterterrorism. In the future, they may struggle to keep up with the vast amount of online information that circulates around the world.

The Hidden Threat

Counterterrorism experts say that terrorists are increasingly using the Internet to communicate with each other and plan their crimes. Unless experts know exactly where they are looking or develop complicated computer systems to do it for them, looking for communications from terrorists is a very difficult task. Because of this, counterterrorism agents are constantly developing new techniques to counter the ever growing "cyber threat."

In the past, terrorists have been caught using computers in Internet cafés to plan their crimes.

Mining for Evidence

There are two cutting-edge techniques experts say will be important in the future: data mining and genetic algorithms. Both are ways of sifting through huge amounts of information to find specific things.

Collecting Data

Data mining and genetic algorithms are already used by some governments. The US government uses data mining to collect information on airline passengers. Some people think that this is a violation of people's right to privacy.

BACK IN THE LAB

Data mining involves collecting huge amounts of information about people and then storing it on computers. This information can be analyzed using software programs called databases. Counterterrorism agents can then use the databases to search for people who fit the profile of suspected terrorists, such as known religious fundamentalists who have been buying plane tickets to and from countries suspected of supporting terrorism.

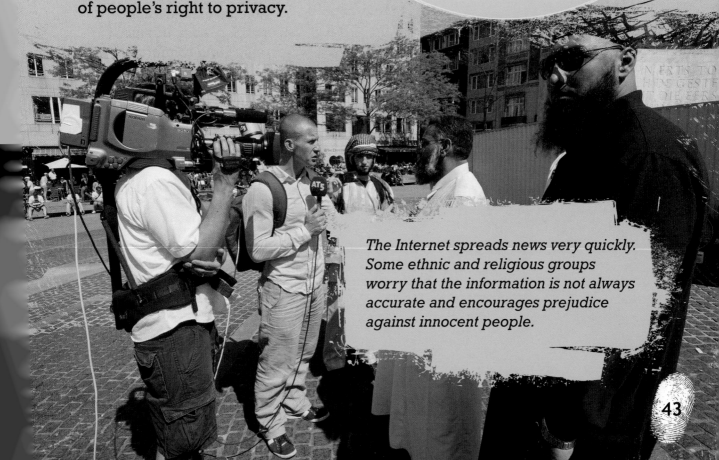

The Internet spreads news very quickly. Some ethnic and religious groups worry that the information is not always accurate and encourages prejudice against innocent people.

CONSTANT BATTLE

Following the events of 9/11, the London bombings of July 2005, and the Mumbai bombings of 2011, we all know just how real the threat of terrorism in the twenty-first century is. As a result, today more resources than ever before are being poured into counterterrorism to keep people safe.

Winning the War

In the last three decades, science has helped tackle terrorism. There have been many successes, from the development of accurate DNA and biometrics tests to the invention of the Global Positioning System and full-body scanners at airports. Through the use of these inventions and others, many terrorists have been arrested and put on trial for their crimes, or stopped before they can carry out their plans. More than ever before, governments are winning the fight against terrorism.

Whenever a terrorist attack occurs, trained police and soldiers must be ready to respond.

The events of 9/11 proved beyond any doubt that terrorism is something that can affect us all.

Into the Future

There are still many challenges ahead for the counterterrorism agents charged with keeping people safe. Finding and monitoring terrorists in the Internet age is becoming increasingly problematic, and there is still much we do not understand about the threat of biological and chemical weapons.

An Ongoing Struggle

Terrorists will never stop plotting new ways to harm people, so counterterrorism scientists must keep working hard to develop new ways to find, stop, and convict them.

REAL-LIFE CASE

In October 2012, Quazi Mohammad Rezwanul Ahsan Nafis was arrested for attempting to blow up the Federal Reserve Bank in New York. FBI agents uncovered his plan after spotting fundamentalist messages he had posted online. They later recorded phone calls from Nafis explaining his plan to an undercover FBI agent.

GLOSSARY

analysis a careful study of something

animal rights activists people who are against any kind of cruelty to animals

biodetector something designed to indicate the presence of a certain germ or chemical

biometrics the science of identifying people by the size and shape of certain body features

ceasefire an arrangement that results in an end to terrorism or another form of military action

compound a number of buildings surrounded by a high wall or fence intended to keep out strangers

computer analyst someone who looks through information held on a computer and analyzes it

data information

database computer software program for collecting and analyzing information (data)

dismantle to take something apart

DNA short for deoxyribonucleic acid, the unique code inside every human body cell that controls every element of how people look, such as the color of their eyes

forensic a detailed study of a particular subject (for example, science, for use in a court of law)

frequency how often something happens

fundamentalist someone with extreme views, sometimes based on a particular interpretation of religious teachings

laboratory any place where scientific testing takes place

microscope a piece of equipment used by scientists to look at incredibly small things that are difficult to see with the naked eye

monitor to watch or keep a close eye on something or someone

nanotechnology a method of creating incredibly small things, such as computer parts or weapons

network a number of objects, for example computers or satellites, which communicate with each other or are in some way connected

notorious well-known

political views opinions on how a country should be governed, or an interest in a particular aspect of government business

prying watching

racist someone who is prejudiced against others because of the color of their skin

satellite a man-made object sent into space to do a specific job (for example, broadcasting television pictures or pinpointing locations)

separatist someone who wishes to create a "separate" country for a particular group of people

software program something on a computer designed to do a specific task

surveillance the process of watching or keeping track of someone using a range of methods, such as listening devices or hidden cameras

traces very small amounts

FOR MORE INFORMATION

BOOKS

Crelinstein, Ronald D. *Counterterrorism*. Malden, MA:
Polity Press, 2009.

Friedman, Mark. *America's Struggle With Terrorism*.
New York, NY: Scholastic, 2011.

Woolf, Alex. *Why Are People Terrorists?* Chicago, IL:
Heinemann-Raintree, 2005.

WEBSITES

Find out more about counterterrorism around the world at:
**academickids.com/encyclopedia/index.php/
Counterterrorism**

*Discover a great introduction to the world of forensic science,
featuring explanations of many of the techniques mentioned
in this book at:*
www.all-about-forensic-science.com

*For details of how you can try some forensic science
techniques at home visit:*
www.explainthatstuff.com/forensicscience.html

*For famous cases, fun with forensics, and explanations of
detailed techniques:*
http://library.thinkquest.org/TQ0312020/

INDEX